EDUCATION FOR SOCIAL WORKERS
IN THE CORRECTIONAL FIELD

Education for Social Workers in the Correctional Field

ELLIOT STUDT

VOLUME V

A Project Report of the Curriculum Study
Werner W. Boehm, Director and Coordinator

COUNCIL ON SOCIAL WORK EDUCATION
345 EAST 46TH STREET, NEW YORK 17, N. Y.

60

Printed in the United States of America
by H. Wolff Book Manufacturing Co., Inc.

PANEL PARTICIPANTS

The affiliations listed are those of the participants at the time of panel membership.

Tessie Berkman
Graduate School of Public Administration and Social Service
New York University
New York, New York

Eleanor G. Cranefield
School of Social Work
University of Michigan
Ann Arbor, Michigan

William G. Nagel
New Jersey Reformatory
Bordentown, New Jersey

Lloyd E. Ohlin
New York School of Social Work
Columbia University
New York, New York

John A. Wallace
Probation Department
Supreme Bench of Baltimore City
Baltimore, Maryland

Irving Weisman
Louis M. Rabinowitz School of Social Work
Hunter College
New York, New York

Corresponding Members

John Conrad
Department of Corrections
Sacramento, California

Maurice F. Connery
School of Social Work
University of Minnesota

Project Director

Elliot Studt, D.S.W.
Graduate School of Social Work
Rutgers University
New Brunswick, New Jersey

PUBLISHER'S NOTE

Board Policy

This project report of the Curriculum Study is published in accordance with the policy adopted by the Board of Directors of the Council at its meeting on October 9–11, 1958. The policy adopted provides that:

The content of Curriculum Study reports are the responsibility of the Curriculum Study staff;

These reports will be published by the Council as submitted to it by the Study staff and given the widest possible distribution;

The Council, through all possible channels, shall encourage thorough consideration and discussion of the findings and recommendations and their implications for social work education and practice.

The Board decided further that:

Publication and distribution of the Curriculum Study reports does not imply Council acceptance of the findings or recommendations;

Implementation of any of the recommendations of the Study can come only after the field has had full opportunity to consider the reports, the appropriate bodies of the Council have considered and recommended action which would modify or change existing policies and standards.

The Board sincerely hopes that the many challenging questions which the Study presents will be given the mature, deliberate and objective consideration they merit and which characterize the true profession.

The Board wishes to register on behalf of the Council its sincere appreciation to the Study staff whose dedicated service brought the Curriculum Study to a successful conclusion.

The thirteen volumes of the Curriculum Study have been numbered to facilitate reference and identification. The comprehensive report has been numbered Volume I, the report on undergraduate education because of its comprehensive nature has been numbered Volume II. The other volumes have been numbered in alphabetical order by title as follows:

Acknowledgments

The Board is pleased to make public acknowledgment of its appreciation to the following foundations and organizations whose grants made possible the financing of this Curriculum Study:

FIELD FOUNDATION

ITTLESON FAMILY FOUNDATION

NATIONAL INSTITUTE OF MENTAL HEALTH, DEPARTMENT OF HEALTH, EDUCATION, AND WELFARE

NATIONAL TUBERCULOSIS ASSOCIATION

NEW YORK FUND FOR CHILDREN

OFFICE OF VOCATIONAL REHABILITATION, DEPARTMENT OF HEALTH, EDUCATION, AND WELFARE

ROCKEFELLER BROTHERS FUND

Although all projects of the Curriculum Study were interdependent and each contributed to the others and to the comprehensive report—and the staff worked as a team under one director—certain grants were more particularly earmarked for designated projects. Accordingly, acknowledgment is made of this circumstance in the appropriate volumes.

In addition to grants from these organizations, the Council on Social Work Education made substantial contributions from its own funds.

—Ernest F. Witte

New York, New York   *Executive Director*

May, 1959   *Council on Social Work Education*

Preface

This comprehensive three-year study of curriculum in the education of social workers has been completed under the auspices of the Council on Social Work Education. It has comprised twelve separate projects, one of which is reported in the following pages.

The twelve individual project reports are published separately by the Council to meet the needs of social work educators and practitioners whose interest is especially concentrated in the subject matter of one or more of the projects. No single report, however, can be understood in its proper relation to the whole study without reference to the comprehensive report, *Objectives for the Social Work Curriculum of the Future,* in which the findings and recommendations of the total study are presented. The various project directors worked together as a staff under the over-all guidance of Dr. Werner W. Boehm, Director and Coordinator of the Curriculum Study. Their goal was not only to develop desirable educational objectives for each project's particular area of the curriculum or suggested by particular considerations of practice, but, in addition, to do so in a way that would merge them all into a total educational experience.

Each project was designed to fit into a master plan for the study of the total curriculum. The findings and recommendations of each are relevant to those of the whole Study and have in turn been influenced by all other projects. To be understood, each report must therefore be considered in relation to the comprehensive report, which it supplements by supplying details for the particular area of the social work curriculum.

WHY THE STUDY WAS UNDERTAKEN

Many issues facing social work education were identified in the
Hollis-Taylor Report of 1951.[1] It confirmed that the great pre-
ponderance of persons engaged in social work activities were still
without professional education. It raised such questions as:

Does social work have a well-defined and identified function?

Does it possess a systematic body of knowledge, skills and attitudes
in the various areas of social work practice?

Is the content of social work education sufficiently well developed so
that it can be transmitted, and is it of such caliber that it can be included properly as a professional discipline within a university?

Progress toward answering these questions was made by the
adoption of the Council's Curriculum Policy Statement in 1952,
but further study was indicated. Social work education had also to
face other issues:

How could it meet the greatly increased need for social work personnel?

How best could it train for a professional practice still in the process
of rapid change and development? Can it be broad enough in scope
to enable social workers to function in fields just emerging as well as
those already established? Will breadth of education to encompass
all fields of professional practice result in dilution of competence for
specific fields?

How could it inculcate qualities of leadership and statesmanship
while at the same time training for competence in specific practice?

Should undergraduate education serve primarily as a basis for graduate training or also prepare personnel for certain social work positions?

The Study considered that materials from which answers to all
these questions might emerge would be obtained by focusing upon

[1] Ernest V. Hollis and Alice L. Taylor, *Social Work Education in the United States*
(New York: Columbia University Press, 1951).

fundamental questions of curriculum planning and not by piece-meal consideration of the specific questions posed. In education for social work as for other professions, the fundamental consid-erations in curriculum planning apply, as presented succinctly by Dr. Ralph W. Tyler.[2] Paraphrased for purposes of this study they are:

What are the desirable educational objectives for professional edu-cation?

What learning experiences should be selected and devised and how organized, to realize these objectives?

What are the effective means of evaluating whether the objectives have been attained?

Without a clear formulation of the objectives of social work edu-cation, that is, the knowledge, skills and attitudes students are expected to acquire, it becomes impossible to plan the learning experiences needed or to evaluate their success. Consequently, the Curriculum Study singled out as its major task identification of the desirable objectives of social work education.

Also, in accordance with Dr. Tyler's definition, each project framed its educational objectives in terms of both the *content* to be covered and the kind and quality of *behavior* to be expected from the student in relation to the content. For example, "famil-iarity" with a certain area of content becomes distinguishable from behaviors involving more complex manipulations or deeper "un-derstanding" of content at other levels of student learning.

HOW THE STUDY WAS CARRIED ON

The individual projects of the study fell into the following major areas:

1. Specific curriculum areas—projects devised to examine the curriculum in the areas identified by the Curriculum Policy Statement of 1952: Human Growth and Behavior, the Social

2 Ralph W. Tyler, *Basic Principles of Curriculum and Instruction* (Chicago: The University of Chicago Press, 1950).

Services, Social Work Methods (casework, group work, community organization, research, administration).
2. Selected fields of practice—projects devised to study elements of practice in rehabilitation, public social services, and corrections.
3. Undergraduate education for social work.
4. Content on social work values and ethics found throughout the curriculum.

Each project was planned to identify educational objectives in existing curricula; to formulate a series of desirable objectives, the desirability of which was determined by judging their importance, consistency and compatibility with a statement of the nature and function of social work; and to review the objectives in the light of educational theory as to the possibility of their being learned in the time and conditions available. Project directors had consultation and assistance from specially selected panels of educators and practitioners in social work and related disciplines.

WHAT THE STUDY HOPES TO ACCOMPLISH

Responsibility for planning and constructing curriculum belongs basically to the social work schools and departments. As a group they have already come far toward definition of common educational goals for the profession and of content all curricula must have to reach such goals. The Curriculum Study is expected to provide guides for the resolution of the major issues and common questions that it is anticipated will arise in the curriculum planning of all member schools and departments of the Council on Social Work Education.

Contents

EDUCATION FOR SOCIAL WORKERS IN THE CORRECTIONAL FIELD

Introduction

METHOD

The report of the Project on Social Work in Corrections is a formulation of the concepts emerging from the work of many organized groups. These groups have operated primarily under the leadership of the Committee on Corrections of the Council on Social Work Education, and have included in their membership faculty members from schools of social work (including persons not directly acquainted with corrections), social work practitioners in corrections, correctional administrators, psychiatrists, and sociologists. Their concern has been to examine afresh the problems of social work practice in corrections, to identify the areas where further study and formulation are needed, and to propose the conceptual framework which offers most for the understanding of correctional social work practice.

Although the members of these groups have been aware of bibliographical sources, the emphasis has been on a new look at practice. Therefore no bibliography is appended. The sources listed at the end of this Introduction refer primarily to the statements which have been developed in the course of the three years' work of the committee and its sub-groups.

The groups which have contributed to the thinking reflected in this report include:

The Council on Social Work Education Committee on Corrections
   Sub-Committee on Theoretical Development
      Regional Work Group on the Nature of the Caseload
      Regional Work Group on the Nature of Treatment
      Regional Work Group on Teamwork in Corrections
      Regional Work Group on Legal Concepts
   Workshop on the Nature of Practice in Correctional Social Work, Council on Social Work Education Annual Program Meeting, Los Angeles, January 1957

The Interdisciplinary Panel on the *Casebook on Correctional Casework,* Los Angeles, February 1957

The Summer Session for Social Work Teachers on Correctional Social Work, University of California at Berkeley, Summer of 1956

Important contributions have been made to conceptual formulations by the findings of the Center for Education and Research in Corrections of the University of Chicago. The Training Branch of the Juvenile Delinquency Services Division of the U.S. Children's Bureau has provided staffing and leadership for many of the projects sponsored by the Committee on Corrections.

The final form of this report has been prepared by the project director while chairman of the Council's Committee on Corrections and Russell Sage Professor at the Rutgers University School of Social Work. The work on the document has been a contribution to the Curriculum Study by the Russell Sage Foundation and the report is in many respects a synopsis of sections of the manuscript being prepared for the Foundation.

SOURCE MATERIALS

Minutes of the Sub-Committee on Theory Development in Correctional Practice, April 19–20, 1956

"Some Basic Concepts Relating to Social Work Practice in Corrections," Summary of Seminar Material, Summer Session for Social Work Teachers on Correctional Social Work, 1956

Report of Workshop on Problems of Practice in Correctional Social Work, January 1957

Regional Work Group Papers:

New York Work Group:	"The Selection of the Juvenile and the Adult Offender"
	"The Acculturation of the Offender:
	A. Community Factors
	B. The Law Enforcement Process
	C. The Correctional Institution"
Northern California	"Social Work in Probation and Parole"

Work Group:	"Correctional Treatment in the Institution"
	"Problems of the Social Worker in the Practice of Correctional Treatment"
Southern California Work Group:	"Central Legal Issues and Concepts for Training for Social Work in Corrections"
Minnesota Work Group:	"Problems in Teamwork in Corrections"

Preliminary Report of the Center for Education and Research in Corrections: *Sociology and the Field of Corrections* by Lloyd E. Ohlin (New York: Russell Sage Foundation, 1956)

CHAPTER I

Functions of Social Workers in the Correctional Field

DEFINITION OF CORRECTIONS

Corrections is a social process by which modern society deals with officially identified lawbreakers. It is administered by a system of diversely organized agencies. The correctional system warrants study as a field of social work practice because the particular configuration of social worker-client roles required by correctional service produces significant adaptations of social work method and skill.

CORRECTIONS AS A SOCIAL PROCESS

Corrections is one of four social processes utilized by modern administration of criminal justice. These are: (1) law enforcement, which is concerned with the collection of evidence about reported offenses and with the detection and arrest of suspected offenders; (2) prosecution and defense, or the preparation and presentation of criminal cases before the court; (3) judicial process, which is concerned with the legal determination of guilt and the assignment of penalties; (4) corrections, which is responsible for administering the assigned penalties.

The modern correctional process developed in the 19th century as the result of major modifications in the penalty system. In the 17th and 18th centuries the primary penalties for lawbreaking were death, mutilation and banishment. These penalties eliminated the offender from the community entirely or branded him permanently as a criminal. The administration of such penalties required only such personnel as the hangman and the keeper of the jail where offenders were held for trial and execution. During the early part of the 19th century one of the many reforms which reflected a new evaluation of human life was the substitution of varying periods of restricted supervised status in the penalty system for capital punishment. Penalties involving time, status and restriction are still punishments by the community, but they maintain the offender as a member of society. Such penalties require a different kind of administrative personnel and an expanded agency structure to supervise these periods of restricted status and to keep track of the way the restrictions are observed and the obligations of the status are discharged.

The modification of the penalty system did more than require a different kind of administrative structure and personnel. It made possible the idea of treatment. Keeping the offender in some sort of defined relationship to the community, and returning him to normal status in the community at the end of the penalty period, inevitably produced concern about the possibility of further offending behavior. Although the first interest was in controlling the offender's behavior during the period of the penalty, there has also been continuing social concern that offenders should somehow be reformed or corrected during the period when they can be observed and controlled. With the increasing knowledge about the dynamics of human behavior and how it is modified, which has become available in the 20th century, it has become possible to give attention to the rehabilitation of the offender. Thus the correctional process has come to mean the administration of the penalty in such a way that the offender is "corrected," *i.e.,* his current behavior is kept within acceptable limits at the same time that his general life adjustment is modified.

Corrections is therefore a social process by which society maintains legally identified offenders as members of the community in temporarily handicapped status. The necessities of this task require both control over the behavior of the offender during the period of his penalty and services designed to help him achieve a less socially dangerous mode of participation in the community.

CORRECTIONS AS A SYSTEM OF OPERATING AGENCIES

The modern correctional process is administered through a system of operating agencies which are a part of the formal system of social control and are authorized to use, under limitations, the force of the state to protect the community against the unlawful acts which might be performed by the offenders in their care. They are primarily governmental agencies, established by legislation which authorizes their activities and makes the service mandatory for both agency and client.

There are two kinds of agencies in the correctional system, each representing a different degree of restriction over the offender. These are the field agencies (probation and parole) and institutions. Probation is supervision of the offender while he lives in the community. It is a substitute for commitment to the institution. Parole is such supervision in the community after the offender has spent a certain part of his penalty period in an institution. Institutions are controlled communities, outside the normal community but related to it, which provide intramural care during a portion of the penalty.

These two types of agencies show great variation in organizational patterns throughout the United States. This diversity seems to result from four major social factors:

There is a strong influence of the locality on correctional organization. Correctional agencies are functionally close to local law enforcement. Enabling legislation tends to be broad, allowing local administrators and their supporting power groups to determine patterns of organization. Urban and rural areas present very different problems to agencies dealing with crime and delinquency. State leadership has been slow to develop and where states have taken responsibility for correctional services they have followed diverse administrative patterns. No supervision over correctional development is provided at the level of federal government.

The reform which separated work with juvenile delinquents from work with adult offenders created a "sub-field" in the correctional system. This change added to the diversity of organizational patterns by which the correctional process is administered. As a few states have set up separate structures for dealing with youthful offenders, still further organizational variations have been introduced.

Correctional services are staffed by personnel from many different educational backgrounds. Until recently there has been little agreement about the education which is appropriate for preparation of different groups of correctional personnel. Different definitions of the purposes of the correctional process have resulted in widely divergent ideas about preferred educational backgrounds. Different academic disciplines and professions have been variously responsive to the educational needs of the correctional field and have affected the kinds of personnel available for employment. The fact that corrections is a basic public service which must be staffed has made it necessary to employ less well-qualified personnel when professionally educated persons could not be recruited.

Corrections is in a period of flux and change with experimental treatment programs existing side by side with relics of the dark ages of corrections. Social purposes of punishment, correction and rehabilitation are all actively expressed in our society and are differently reflected in the decisions of different correctional administrators. Many agencies have been charged with treatment responsibilities without provision of the necessary resources. In a period such as this it can be expected that agencies will differ from each other in definition of the correctional process, in kinds of responsibilities accepted, in organizational patterns, and in structural relationships with other agencies in the community.

In spite of diversity in detail the general characteristics of the correctional system can be described as follows:

THE CORRECTIONAL CASELOAD

The correctional caseload is composed of officially identified offenders each of whom has been assigned a handicapped status as the penalty for his offense.

The legal handicaps in this status include: loss of civil rights; special and continued jeopardy as to further loss of liberty; limitations on rights of privacy; limitations on freedom to act in specified areas without approval; limitations on mobility, including the obligation to remain in contact with his supervising officer.

The social and personal handicaps resulting from this status include: handicaps in case of access to social organizations such as military services, schools, and employing organizations; handicaps deriving from the community perception of the offender, which is handicapping whether it be rejection by the middle class part of the community or increased prestige with the delinquent sub-culture; handicaps arising from the modification of the offender's self-image, which are again handicapping whether the self-image is modified in the direction of shame or pride.

Offenders who are committed to correctional agencies are selected by social processes from a much larger population of actual law-

breakers. Factors which enter into this social selection process include: lack of resources on the part of the offender and his family; the special jeopardy of the individual who has been previously designated an offender; the practices of local law enforcement; public concern about certain crimes; the inadequacies of law; and many others.

As a result of these social selection processes the correctional caseload is made up of the least adequate offenders. It includes very few white collar criminals, professional criminals, or members of organized criminal gangs. Persons who are assigned to the correctional caseload tend to be "difficulty prone," lacking in social and personal resources, evasive and unskilled in dealing with community services, impulsive, and lacking in the basic skills essential to the acceptable performance of social roles such as parent, student, and employe. Many correctional clients are the failures of previous social agency efforts; they do not voluntarily seek help and may have to be held within a mandatory relationship if they are to be served. They come in large proportion from lower economic groups and express the sub-culture of these groups. Many are part of delinquent sub-cultures and become part of correctional sub-cultures.

Since crime and delinquency are legally defined behaviors, not all officially identified offenders can be classified as mentally or emotionally ill. The offending behavior of some individuals is primarily a response to situational factors. Some develop progressively severe maladjustments in response to the stresses experienced in the correctional process as it is administered. A small proportion present clinically recognizable neuroses and psychoses. A much larger number fall into a large and little studied classification of "acting-out disorders."

The correctional caseload includes juveniles, youth and adults. Juveniles are included in the correctional caseload whenever their behavior has been defined by law as delinquency and a supervised status has been assigned. The differences between the juvenile caseload and the adult caseload lie in the modification of procedures for handling the younger age group, the different implications of the handicapped status for the person who is already a legal minor, and the different problems and potentialities of the young person's developmental period. Delinquency as legally defined is primarily a phenomenon of adolescence rather than of childhood, and self-identification as a delinquent and social dangerousness are as characteristic of juvenile as of adult offenders.

The correctional situations of juvenile, youthful and adult offenders are similar in basic characteristics.

The correctional caseload is largely a male population.

SOCIAL WORK ROLES IN THE CORRECTIONAL SYSTEM

Corrections is a multi-discipline field and requires personnel from all the professions along with many technical personnel. Job descriptions in the correctional bureaucracy have developed by combining functionally related operations rather than according to the roles described by the professions. However, in the bureaucratic process of organizing functions into jobs, certain positions have emerged which roughly correspond to social work roles. At this point in correctional history most of these jobs are defined as casework positions.

In the field services the main body of personnel are probation and parole officers who discharge the primary responsibility of the agency. They serve as officers of a court or parole board and are thus responsible for communicating information to judicial or quasi-judicial bodies and for administering their orders. They also supervise offenders in the community and are thus responsible for individualizing control plans according to the needs of each client, for offering counseling service, and for working with those persons and agencies in the community who are affected by and who affect the adjustment of the client.

The positions of probation officer and parole officer as now designed are close to the professional definition of casework. Particular jobs in probation and parole may include technical tasks such as checking arrest reports and transporting offenders to institutions. However, most of the time of a probation or parole officer is spent in activities which affect the offender's attitudes and his relationships with his community and its agencies.

The positions by which social workers enter employment in correctional institutions comprise only a small proportion of the positions necessary to institutional administration, and rarely approximate the full scope of the possible social work role. Rather, each such position may emphasize one or another aspect of social work functioning. They may be known by such titles as classification officer, institutional parole officer, treatment worker, diagnostic clinic worker, or supervisor of cottage life. It is characteristic of the social work task in the correctional institution that the worker may need to engage the administrator in identifying needed services and in reformulating job descriptions so that the institution may benefit from a fuller use of social work skills.

In all the correctional services, both institutional and field, the value of group services to offenders is increasingly recognized so that positions for group workers are being created and caseworkers are offering certain group services.

At this point in the development of correctional services, the career line of the professional social worker tends to show rapid movement into research, demonstration, and administrative positions. Thus positions which may not call for social work background in the job specifications, such as those of institutional superintendents, associate wardens in prisons, chief probation officers, and directors of parole are often filled by graduate social workers who, because of the combination of education and experience, have become qualified for strategic leadership.

Closely related to correctional social work jobs are positions which offer services to offenders at earlier points in the law enforcement and judicial processes. Such positions may be found in police departments, in detention homes and jails, and in prosecuting attorneys' offices. There are a number of positions, particularly in juvenile probation work, which combine basic services to families and children with correctional services to delinquents. Other positions sometimes included in the correctional field but less identified with the basic correctional processes are those which serve civil courts in making decisions about family matters such as adoptions and custody. Certain groups of personnel whose activities are closely related to corrections are found in the private agencies whose primary function is to serve identified offenders and in the agencies which accept referral of adjudicated delinquents along with children with other problems.

THE CORRECTIONAL SYSTEM IN THE ADMINISTRATION OF CRIMINAL JUSTICE

All correctional agencies are functionally interrelated with the other agencies of criminal justice. This fact affects every aspect of the correctional agency from the way its organizational structure is designed to the decision making of each correctional officer as he deals with the individual offender. Thus probation departments are responsible for gathering information to be used in making judicial decisions. Institutional workers contribute to the material needed by semi-judicial bodies in making parole decisions. Probation and parole officers share with the police the control of offenders in the community. And a prosecuting attorney may share with the probation or parole officer the decision as to whether a new offense is to be treated as a violation of probation or parole or taken to court for adjudication. All correctional personnel serve the other processes of criminal justice through sharing records and decisions, while they assume primary responsibility for the correctional process.

SOCIAL CHANGE PROCESSES IN THE CORRECTIONAL SYSTEM

The correctional system is in a period of social change which has been made possible by the accomplishments of the last 150 years. These accomplishments include:

> The implementation of a doctrine of equality before the law regardless of class or economic status.
> The use in the penalty system of various periods of restricted supervised status in substitution for the punishments of death, mutilation and banishment.
> Differentiation among offenders on the basis of age and mental competence for the determination of criminal responsibility and disposition.
> Provision of supervision in the community (probation and parole) for selected offenders instead of uniform institutionalization.
> Differentiation among institutions for different classes of offenders.
> Modification of institutions in various ways which might contribute to the reform of individual offenders.

In the accomplishing of such tasks the focus of leaders has necessarily been on social action, legislative reform and administrative invention. The skills necessary for the kind of treatment of offenders which is made possible by these forms of organization have as yet been given less attention. However, progressive adoption of these measures has resulted in an increased social demand that agencies make good on the promise of rehabilitation implied in the new forms of organization. The present historically necessary task of the corrections field is to define the nature of rehabilitative treatment for offenders, to develop the structure for such treatment and to prepare the personnel to man such services.

Because social work is a discipline with a formulated body of knowledge and skills specifically concerned with the modification of the social functioning of individuals, it is one of the professions with a potential contribution to make to the professionalization of correctional service. The nature of the present social task is requiring change in the correctional system. It also requires a changed and change-producing relationship between the field of corrections and the social work profession.

CORRECTIONS AS A FIELD OF SOCIAL WORK PRACTICE

In the system of correctional agencies the social worker and his client are related in a configuration of reciprocal roles. These are:

A social worker legally responsible for both generalized control over and service to clients;

Clients who are clients because they are officially identified lawbreakers.

Social work practice within this role configuration evidences certain characteristic adaptations of methods and skill. Although aspects of these roles occur in many areas of social work service, social work in the administration of the correctional process is the one example of practice where this configuration of roles in its entirety is central to giving service. Corrections can therefore be defined as a field of social work practice and appropriately studied in order to identify the central concepts which govern the necessary professional adaptations. Such formulation of concepts contributes to the general development of social work theory and has implications for social work education.

THE TASKS OF SOCIAL WORKERS
IN CORRECTIONS

THE BASIC TASKS

Social workers enter employment in the correctional system as probation or parole officers and in various positions in correctional institutions. The tasks of social workers in these various positions can be summarized as follows:

1. *Act as the officer of the court or other quasi-judicial body to investigate and report on the offender and his social situation, contributing the results of such social studies in an appropriate and meaningful way to the making of legal decisions.*

2. *Supervise the client's social activities in such a way that:*
   Violations of the conditions of his status and his success in meeting conditions are perceived and can be reported.
   The general control plan provided in the status is individualized according to the client's need for constructive social control.
   Controls are provided by the worker in such a way that the client is supported in viably conforming behavior and inner growth toward self-control is stimulated.

3. *Help the involuntary client to:*
   Handle the stresses produced by the law enforcement and correctional process constructively.
   Become motivated to ask for and use help in problem solving.
   Modify his behavior in the direction of increasingly viable conformity with social expectations.

4. *As the formal authority person in the client's life, work with other authorities associated with the client (parents, teachers, employers, social agencies, institutional personnel) in such a way that:*
   The problems of these authorities with the client are alleviated.
   The activities of the authorities support the client's efforts toward satisfactory behavior.
   The client is more soundly linked with the resources of his groups and his community.

5. *Administer a caseload or group load in such a way that:*
The worker's decisions are appropriate and responsible.

The decisions of other personnel in the administration of criminal justice are respected, implemented, and appropriately influenced by the social worker's knowledge.

The necessities of legal and administrative deadlines are observed.

The emergencies in the lives of clients are met with full attention to their significance for change.

6. *Enact a role in a multidiscipline agency involving shared decisions and teamwork obligations in partnership with:*
Personnel from other professions.

Personnel in the same role as his but with other educational backgrounds.

Personnel with sub-professional assignments and backgrounds.

Personnel from other agencies in the administration of criminal justice.

Personnel in other correctional agencies who have served the client or will in the future.

7. *Take a responsible part in the social change of his agency and in the development of the field of service to which his agency belongs, contributing from his professional knowledge and experience to the determination of policy.*

8. *Contribute to the developing professional knowledge of social work in corrections.*

In order to discharge these tasks the correctional social worker needs generic social work education. The basic structure of social work practice with its processes of study, diagnosis, evaluation, and planned work directed to helping individuals, groups, and communities solve problems is inherent in these tasks as in any social work job. Special knowledges, skills and attitudes required for competence in correctional social work are best discovered by examining the implications for social work practice of the role configuration which is unique to corrections. These implications are identified by noting those correctional tasks which create problems of adaptation for professionally educated social workers.

CORRECTIONAL TASKS REQUIRING ADAPTATIONS IN SOCIAL WORK PRACTICE

Not all the adaptations of social work practice in corrections can be considered in this report. The correctional tasks requiring adaptation which have been selected for discussion are those which have been consistently reported as presenting problems to graduate social workers employed in the correctional field. They are also the correctional tasks which the profession has questioned as a part of the social worker's role. The problem tasks to be considered are:

1. *Investigation and surveillance for the purpose of securing information about the client's failures or successes in meeting the obligations of his legal status.* This is a version of the process of social study, but has special aspects in dealing with the involuntary client, whose liberty may be further restricted on the basis of such a study, and whose privacy is legally limited. There are also special skills involved in reporting such social studies so that they can serve both the needs of the judicial decision-making process and the needs of the treatment process.

2. *The use of controls to modify client behavior.* This again is part of the commonly recognized process of professional control but extends to the use by the social worker of controls which are based on the force of the state and which impinge on a wider area of personal functioning than is characteristic of other social work assignments.

3. *Acting as a legal authority person in the client's life with responsibility for value change.* This task has important implication for the treatment relationship. These implications are observed particularly in the transference components which characteristically appear in the initial stages of the correctional relationship and in the group supported defenses which are mobilized when value change is the goal of treatment.

4. *Correctional decision-making.* It is recognized that all social workers make decisions. There are, however, aspects in decision-making in correctional work which require adaptations by the professional social worker. These seem to lie in the nature of

the decisions to be made, the structure of decision-making, and the lack of resources on which the social worker is accustomed to depend in making decisions.

In order to explore these tasks as part of social work roles and the adaptations which they require, the following questions have been asked:

What is the nature of the tasks?
Why do they present problems of adaptation for graduate social workers?
What needs—of system or of client—do these tasks satisfy?
Can they be seen as appropriate tasks for the professional social worker and in what way?

It is evident in the following analyses that the profession has only begun to break ground in answering these questions. It has been possible to indicate the nature of the difficulties and to establish the relationship of each task to social work responsibility for treatment. Directions in which further study is necessary have also been identified.

1. *Investigation and Surveillance*

Somebody in correctional services has to observe, assess and report whether the client is meeting the obligations of his legal status.
Is this task properly part of the professional social work task? Three functions are served by this activity:

Gathering information needed by the system in order to make decisions.
Developing for each client an individualized diagnostic formulation which will determine the nature of the control and treatment plan.
Providing one aspect of control over the client since he tends to modify his behavior when he is aware that there is efficient observation of his activities.

Social workers have tended to reject the observational activities required in this task because it involves taking initiative to discover facts in areas which the client does not want observed and may lead to decisions about actions which are disliked by the client. However, in each of these functions, services are performed for the community, the system, and the clients. The community benefits when clients are handled appropriately on the basis of sufficient information which will allow appropriate decision-making; the client benefits when his needs are understood and controls and treatment are appropriately designed.

Although anyone in the correctional job may be able to collect and report information, it takes a high degree of professional social work skill to select the significant information, to evaluate it so that an appropriate control and treatment plan can be designed, and to report it so that it serves the necessities of both legal and professional decisions. It also takes skill to make the investigative process itself helpful in getting the client started in treatment and to make it a part of the over-all control process. Furthermore, the skill with which the investigation itself is undertaken determines how much and what kind of information will be available.

For all these reasons, but with special emphasis on the skill required to make the investigative process into a restorative experience for the client, the basic investigative tasks now integrated into probation, parole, and institutional classification jobs are accepted as appropriately part of social work tasks in corrections.

2. *The Use of Controls*

Somebody in correctional services has to administer the controls established in the handicapped status of the client and needed by most correctional clients if their behavior is to remain within socially acceptable bounds. It should be noted that in probation and parole the social worker is assigned primary responsibility for administration of controls. In the institution the social worker shares in the control responsibility while custody staff administer the basic control processes. Is such control of behavior a proper function of the social worker and therefore appropriately organized within the role which he occupies?

Some of the controls which the correctional social worker uses and which are not usually integrated into social work roles can be noted:

Making a decision to request revocation of probation or parole.

Reporting to the appropriate judicial or administrative bodies behavior which constitutes violation of rules.

Administering the rules governing the client's handicapped status and recommending the penalties which follow disobedience to the rules.

Recommending action on parole to parole boards.

Making unscheduled home visits.

Performing an arrest.

Social workers have tended to resist the use of such controls as a part of professional functioning for several reasons. These controls are designed to restrict mobility rather than to encourage freedom of action. They have a history of punitive use. They are disliked by the client and for this reason, as well as because they emphasize the greater power and authority of the social worker, they tend to produce distance in the relationship between worker and client. As a result many social workers have insisted on a structural separation between the treatment role and responsibility for administering controls over behavior.

The professional resistance to the use of controls stems in some part from the history of social work. In its early days the relief check was often used to control client behavior in ways not appropriate to or sanctioned by the necessities of the service. As the profession developed there was a strong swing against managing the client and professional functioning was identified with the process of freeing the client to determine his own way of life. The person who "uses controls" was confused with "the person who gains satisfaction through controlling," and in the effort to avoid punitive controls or those used for the satisfaction of the worker an attitude developed of "being against controls." Furthermore case histories as used in teaching have often shown the client's suffering as attributable to the harmful use of controls by parents and other authority persons in the past, leaving the social worker in the position of one who should assuage the traumas of the past by providing the client with a permissive non-controlling experience.

It should be noted that the use of certain controls is a part of all professional social work activity. These controls structure the client's experience and are expressed through certain uses of the relationship, as well as by setting appointments, using intake procedures, and applying eligibility requirements. Controls over behavior can be conceptualized as occurring over a range. This range proceeds from sensitive use of relationship to redirect the client's attention, through determining the patterns by which service will be given, to the more overt controls over behavior which are based on the force of the state. The first part of this range is incorporated into all social work practice to greater or lesser extent, with each kind of practice using its own constellation of controls. The correctional social worker has responsibility for an extended range of controls which includes some *but not all* of the means by which the restrictive force of the state is applied. There are still further controls by force which do not belong to the functioning of the social worker in corrections but which are reserved for the police or for those in the institution who are primarily responsible for secure holding.

The rationale for including certain control activities in the role to be occupied by the social worker rests on the facts of the task:

The caseload is composed of acting-out clients who characteristically need some modification of the normal control structure if they are to behave in a socially tolerable fashion.

The use of controls is often the action which communicates with the clients in a way verbalization never could. It establishes with these clients the strength of the worker so that they are able to respect the worker and lean upon him for help.

The use of controls in correctional service has major impact on the client, and the way they are used determines whether or not treatment becomes possible.

Experiencing proper use of control may be for many clients the major reeducational or treatment aspect of the correctional experience.

It takes great skill to use controls so that the client is encouraged to move toward increased acceptance of responsibility for himself.

Control functions become a significant treatment tool when certain aspects of control are integrated in the service of the professional treatment person.

Therefore the control aspects of probation, parole and institutional social work should remain in the tasks accepted by social workers in corrections because:

a. Controls over behavior must be exercised by someone in the correctional service.
b. The way controls are exercised has a tremendous impact on the client, determining in large measure how he uses treatment.
c. Treatment and control functions can be mediated toward a common professional goal when certain controls are included in the role responsibility of the correctional social worker.

It is recognized that there are many technical problems in the professional use of controls which have not been examined by the profession and are therefore not yet integrated in the education of social workers. Questions which must be studied further include:

How does the worker avoid being forced by the client into a position where because he uses controls the client perceives him as "one of the enemy?"

According to what principles can the worker use controls selectively? How does the worker learn to use only the degree and kind of control which is necessary? How can the worker learn to differentiate the impact of control measures on different types of offenders?

How does the worker deal with the problem of the diminishing efficacy of controls, since practice shows that progressive severity in the use of controls may be necessary in order to maintain acceptable behavior?

How does the worker progressively return control to the client as he demonstrates increased ability to take responsibility for himself?

3. *Acting as the legal authority person in the client's life with responsibilities for value change*

Four areas have been identified in which the treatment relationship is modified in correctional social work by the fact that the worker is a legal authority in the client's life:

The choice of appropriate treatment approaches.

The transference components appearing in the early stages of the relationship.

The group-supported nature of the defenses against treatment.
The shared control over the treatment of the client.

The Choice of Appropriate Treatment Approaches

Two challenges have been made by social workers as to the possibility of providing social work treatment from the position of the authority person who controls behavior and who is responsible for value change. These are that:

> Client growth under treatment is not possible because the regression and acting out which accompanies beginning treatment cannot be allowed under the system. It is too dangerous for client and society to allow him to "get worse before he gets better." Therefore he cannot make use of treatment for growth.
>
> The authority role of the worker cuts him off from necessary diagnostic information which could be obtained in a more neutral situation in which the client would feel free to share significant information about himself.

Both of these challenges arise from a definition of treatment which emphasizes uncovering processes followed by reintegration and which deemphasizes those treatment approaches focused on maintaining and strengthening adaptive patterns. Such a definition of treatment tends to confuse the concept of "therapy" with that of "therapeutic intervention."

It is clear that when the worker in corrections asks himself "what am I and the client together for?" he perceives that he is in a relationship in which working to maintain and strengthen adaptive patterns is the treatment approach of choice. This is true not only because most of his clients are "acting-outers" but also because the client correctly perceives the worker as a super-ego person who is an integral part of the social structure designed to support values. Worker and client are together in order to help the client avoid breaking the law. The fact that client and worker are brought together for this particular task will in itself tend to determine the kind of relationship which will be helpful and the treatment techniques which are appropriate. Using this sort of treatment relationship requires the same knowledge of human dynamics as do other kinds of treatment relationships and requires great skill to keep the relationship focused on adaptation while the worker remains aware of the many complex unverbalized factors which are operating but not directly treated.

If this is a correct definition of the treatment situation in corrections and of the treatment methods of choice in such a situation, then the problem of appropriate information for diagnosis becomes less troublesome. Not all information is necessary for every kind of treatment. Diagnostically significant information is always information which helps answer the question "what should the worker do?" Although information obtainable only through uncovering processes is necessary for treatment designed to work in the area of the unconscious, the importance of such information for understanding what to do in the correctional treatment situation can be questioned. Experience shows that whatever it is important to know about the client in order to decide what to do in this situation can be obtained in the authority role by talking with the client, by observing client behavior and by tapping other sources of information such as observation of the interactions of other persons with the client. There needs to be more work on what information is diagnostically essential in this treatment situation and on devising means by which it can be obtained.

The Transference Components Appearing in the Early Stages of the Relationship

The treatment relationship between worker and client in corrections tends to be characterized by the intense negative transference components which appear in the early stages of the relationship. These are to be differentiated from the transference components appearing in the relationship at a later stage of treatment, which are found to be more similar to those appearing in any social work treatment. At the beginning point, however, the correctional client brings expectations and perceptions to his beginning work with the new authority figure which are characterized by fear of the worker's magical destructive power and by need to become totally dependent on this power. The transference components of the relationship at this point are particularly primitive and the way they are dealt with at the beginning is crucial for all following treatment.

In learning to handle the transference components of the initial stage of the relationship, the worker needs to keep in mind two aspects which characterize them. One is that, although these feelings and expectations are derived from the client's relationships with parents, they have been activated and systematized in a series of stress experiences with other authority figures, some of them quite recent as in arrest, interrogation, detention, and court hearing. It is these later aspects of the transference components to which the worker will need to give immediate attention because the client's feelings about the worker will be in terms of these experiences.

A second factor to be kept in mind is that these client expectations of the worker are culturally supported. Even if the client has had no previous reality experience with members of the "crime-controlling system" he will bring to the experience with the worker expectations about how any member of this system will behave. He has picked up these preconceptions not only from his own group but also from mass communication media and from the stereotypes in our culture.

The experience of successful social workers in corrections is that when this initial stage of the relationship is properly handled succeeding stages of treatment may be little plagued with some of the later "resistances" which appear in work with the voluntary client. Experience has also shown that many social workers new to corrections are hesitant about how to get started in the beginning stages of this sort of relationship, and so compound the difficulties of the later stages of treatment for themselves and the clients.

The Group-Supported Nature of the Defenses Against Treatment

Social workers have long been conscious of the serious defenses against change which correctional clients bring to the treatment situation. The difficult nature of these defenses has been attributed to the authority position of the worker and to the fact that the client has not asked for help. It is useful to note, however, that another factor enters into defenses against treatment or change. This factor may also appear in more social work situations than the profession has heretofore noted, particularly in all types of institutions, and possibly among other client groups such as public assistance clients. However, in corrections, both in institutions and in the field services, the client has a strong sense of belonging to an outcast group by reason of being a client. Further, he realizes that the group to which he belongs is mobilized against allowing its members to be changed by treatment.

The intensity of this factor in correctional client defenses can be attributed in large part to the role definition of worker and client. Defenses against treatment are always mobilized when the client perceives himself and is perceived as "one who is to be changed." When this definition of role takes on the aspect of "values to be changed" his group memberships are automatically involved, since value is a group phenomenon and all human beings find it possible to relate most easily with those who share common values with them. Thus the definition of the client role as "one whose values are to be changed" opposes the client's need to change to his need for group support and creates the preconditions for mobilizing collective defenses, bringing out a group response which insulates the individual against treatment. Social work needs to have more to say about how to work with a person who brings this kind of collective opposition to what the worker is attempting to do, if there is to be genuinely effective social work treatment in corrections.

It is recognized that there are differences between the group supported defenses against treatment in the institution and those in the field services. In the institution the fact that the individual client has to live at close range with others who have been assigned to membership in his "group" means that he is especially dependent on group approval not only for fellowship but often also for his safety. Thus group control over the individual in the institution is strong, and the problem of affecting inmate culture so that it supports individual value change is crucial in institutional treatment. In the field services the client may not be directly related to the other clients; therefore group control over the individual is more diffuse. However, he tends to feel akin to other correctional clients because of the similar handicapped status which society has assigned to all of them, and he is often a member of groups which actually see him in a position of prestige because of his status as an identified offender. More needs to be done to devise ways of modifying the groups to which the offender belongs in order to provide him with group support for value change.

The Sharing of Control Over the Treatment of the Offender

One of the factors affecting the worker-client relationship in corrections is the fact that, since the worker is part of a larger authority structure, all treatment reflects the decisions of other responsible officers, whose education, goals and functions may be quite different from what of the worker. A number of these persons, such as police, judges, and institutional staff, may be in direct contact with the client along with the worker. This factor has implications for the treatment relationship which have not yet been sufficiently explored.

4. Decision Making

One of the common experiences reported by the social worker newly employed in corrections is the increase in the number of serious decisions which he has to make independently. There seem to be several sources for the increased emphasis on decision-making activity in correctional social work.

Close professional *supervision is usually not available.* This is not only because the supervisor may not have professional social work education and is overburdened administratively. It also has to do with the fact that the worker is often out in the field dealing with emergencies which have to be handled on the spot.

These *decisions are often of major importance* to client and to the community, affecting both the client's freedom and the community's safety.

The *"visibility" of these decisions is high* since the activities of offenders are particularly newsworthy. Furthermore, the feelings of all concerned in any decision are usually intense and often hostile and punitive.

Decisions usually involve acting on "calculated risks" since criteria for decisions have not been systematically identified.

Accountability for decisions is highly organized and tightly controlled, since most decisions concern the safety of society and may have to be justified in court.

The worker is held accountable for his decisions by others who share control over the client. These other decision-makers are not, as in the psychiatric setting, persons with overlapping education and competence who can provide consultation about social work decisions; rather they are persons with backgrounds and skills in law, police work, custody, etc. Therefore, the professional social worker is responsible for making his own decisions while adjusting and interpreting them in line with the decisions of persons with quite different backgrounds, goals and functions.

While the social worker has been trained to help the client make his own decisions, he is dealing in corrections with a caseload of clients from whom responsibility for many normal decisions has been removed. Thus he has the experience of making *decisions which he would ordinarily expect to leave with the client,* such as giving permission to move, approving the purchase of a car, etc.

These characteristics of decision-making in correctional social work lead to a continuous focus on the making of decisions in work with the client. Who can make what decisions and why, what decisions the client can and must make for himself, and education of the client in the share of responsible decision-making determine the content of many correctional social work interviews. The way the worker handles his own decision-making responsibilities communicates to the client the nature of helpful authority. The worker's awareness of the decision-making process and use of it as a treatment tool has much to do with the effectiveness of his relationship with correctional clients.

This analysis of tasks in correctional social work which require professional adaptation reveals that each of these tasks serves not only system needs but also client needs. Furthermore, it has become clear that the way these tasks are administered determines how the client uses treatment. Since these are the functions of the correctional process toward which the client feels the greatest initial resistance, special skill is required to administer these tasks so that the client is helped to engage himself in the restorative process. Because of the crucial effect of each of these tasks on the client's ability to use treatment, it seems necessary that the social worker be in a role which allows him to individualize the impact of these functions on the client. In such a role these tasks become tools for treatment and an essential part of case management.

There are many unexplored problem areas in such a professional role. However, in accepting that the professional social worker must integrate treatment and control functions in one professional role if he is to be a competent practitioner in correctional service, a step of importance has been taken toward delineating the knowledge, skill and attitudes he requires to do the job. Some of this knowledge and skill is still to be identified, understood and formulated for educational uses. But at this point a tentative outline of the knowledge, skills and attitudes necessary for competence in correctional social work can be attempted.

GENERAL EDUCATIONAL OBJECTIVES IMPLIED IN THE TASKS

In general, the social worker in corrections requires:

Knowledge of corrections as one of the fields of public social service, with understanding of its historical development, legal base, agency structure, central professions, functions of various personnel, community and agency interrelationships, and major policy issues.

Knowledge of the offender caseload including: the social and personal problems leading to crime and delinquency; the social selection process involved in official identification of offenders; the common stress experiences characteristic of this intake process; the personality disorders represented in the caseload; and the sub-cultures characteristic of this group.

Skills in: working as a member of the criminal justice team; motivating the involuntary client; using authority for making decisions and for exerting controls over behavior as part of treatment; working with the constellation of persons in the family and in the community who are related to the client in each case; contributing to the process of change in the development of services in his agency.

Attitudes of: patience, perspective, flexibility and readiness to act arising from understanding of the field, its tasks and the people with whom it deals, and requiring resolution of personal problems with authority.

CHAPTER II

Educational Objectives:
The Content and Behaviors Desirable
for Social Work Practice in Corrections

THE CONCEPTUAL FRAMEWORK

The first chapter is a description of the factors determining the nature of social work practice in corrections. In order to communicate the essence of such practice through educational processes, the central concepts which organize and give meaning to it must be identified. These concepts must be of such an order that they both illuminate the special contribution of the correctional field to social work theory and provide bridges for generalization to all social work practice.

This part of the report is limited and focused by certain factors:

It presents a series of propositions which up to this date have proved useful in organizing the empirical facts of correctional social work practice. Systematic examination of social work practice in corrections is a comparatively recent development. Its findings are now ready for wide examination, testing and reformulation, but it is clear that many steps must be taken to achieve an inwardly consistent body of concepts which is also fully integrated into generic social work theory.

The inquiry which has resulted in these propositions has been inductive rather than deductive and has focused on problem areas. The method of work has been to ask graduate social workers in the correctional field to identify in their own practice the adaptations of generic social work required by their experience. In this endeavor the basic concepts of generic social work have been assumed as given. Therefore, the following list of concepts is neither inclusive of all the social worker in corrections needs to know, nor is it exclusive in the sense that no other social workers need to understand this material. It does, however, provide a general framework for understanding the special characteristics of correctional social work practice.

This report is based primarily on the practice of casework in corrections. Most present social work practice in corrections is in casework positions. Since the emerging practice of group work in corrections is less generally formulated, it has been necessary to draw heavily on casework both for generic concepts and for evidence of adaptations. Preliminary discussions with group workers who know correctional practice indicate that this conceptual framework is useful for group work as well as for casework, and that group work has an important contribution to make for understanding all social work practice in corrections.

Within the limitations and focus of the presentation, this list of concepts can be used as a provisional framework for the formulation of educational objectives in the preparation of social workers who will be as ready at graduation to enter correctional employment as they are to undertake any other form of social work practice.

CORE CONCEPTS AND EDUCATIONAL OBJECTIVES

DEVIANCE

Delinquent and criminal behavior can be best understood as one form of deviance which brings clients to the attention of remedial services. The behavior which falls within this class of deviance is defined by law. In general, the behavior is either a refusal to accept the obligations of certain core values of our society or an overt attack on these values. These core values relate primarily to security of persons and property, and to sexual behavior.

The social response to this form of deviance is severe and highly structured. The values attacked by this behavior are considered basic obligations of all citizens and have been formulated in a body of criminal law with penalties provided for violations. Because of the feelings which violations of these laws arouse in the members of society, organized processes are required for channeling actions toward the offender. These processes provide substitutes for private vengeance in public legal procedures which protect the rights of the offender and of the community; make public reaffirmation of value as a deterrent to potential offenders; protect the community from further attack by the known offender; and attempt to correct the identified offender through helping him achieve a more acceptable mode of participation within the community.

One characteristic of this form of deviance is that the patterns of the behavior are learned. The techniques of most crimes and delinquencies are passed on through group and individual associations; along with associated patterns for dealing with authorities, they form a large part of the knowledge and skill which is necessary if a person is to maintain himself as this kind of a deviant.

The causation of such deviant behavior varies from offender to offender. For some offenders the central causative factor seems to lie in the way values have been transmitted to them through parents, social institutions, and peers. Many commit such acts because of the role-expectations of groups which are meaningful to them. For many the attack on values is rooted in accumulated deprivations, demands for accomplishment which have been unaccompanied by associated means for achievement, and actual injustices. Other offenders express personality distortions symbolically through criminal acts. There are some for whom the act seems to be a situational response rather than a consistent way of life. The procedures by which society deals with delinquent or criminal behavior are often themselves a causative factor in later offenses. The causation of delinquent and criminal behavior can best be conceptualized in terms of social and psychological strains which impinge differentially on different personalities and on persons in different social strata.

The means for modifying the social functioning of such deviants are various. The models for treatment range from complete psychoanalysis to the most rigid and physically unpleasant prison regime. The tendency in corrections has been to consider one treatment model uniformly applicable to all offenders, regardless of the nature of the behavior and its causation. Because this form of deviance lies in the realm of social relationships and because both social and psychological factors interact in causation, social work would seem to have a major contribution to make to the design of treatment methods.

Because of the complexities of causation and the widely varying models for treatment, the diagnostic appraisal of individuals within this class of deviants and the criteria for measuring success in treatment are less well formulated than in many other social services.

The social worker who would be effective in work with offenders in the correctional caseload will need:

Knowledge of:
Delinquent and criminal behavior as one form of deviance;
The psychological and social strains which in various constellations press individuals toward such behavior;
The body of techniques which is learned by the offender in order to commit offenses and to protect himself in dealings with community authorities;
The diagnostic approaches now in use and the problems inherent in applying them to the correctional caseload.

Skills in:
Identifying the social as well as psychological strains effective in the causation of offending behavior;
Modifying the offender's environment so that strains toward conformity are substituted for those which press toward criminal deviance;
Observing and blocking the use of criminal techniques;
Reeducating the offender in more acceptable techniques for satisfying his needs and for dealing with community representatives;
Setting goals and evaluating progress in individual cases realistically in the light of the nature of the difficulties and the present state of knowledge about treatment and its outcome;
Distilling from his experience with cases the information and insights which the profession must have in order to develop sound treatment methods.

Attitudes of:
Acceptance of delinquent and criminal deviants without condoning anti-social behavior;
Scientific interest in the contributions of social structure to causation and treatment as well as in psychological determinants;
Readiness to work experimentally and without undue discourage-

ment in a field where present knowledge is limited, prognosis is uncertain, and failures frequent.

SOCIAL SELECTION OF CASELOAD

Not all human beings who evidence a certain kind of deviance become clients of a social agency charged with responsibility for dealing with their problems. The social processes by which certain persons are selected from a given deviant population for treatment by a particular social agency are various and have significant consequences for the kinds of problems presented to the service and for the client's feelings about receiving service. The social processes by which certain offenders are selected for correctional treatment from all those persons who commit delinquent and criminal acts are both informal and procedural and are particularly crucial in determining the nature of correctional services.

The operation of the social selection processes to determine which offenders are committed to correctional agencies can be illustrated by an inverted pyramid whose base line is the number of offenses actually reported to the police. Between the commission of offenses and the arrest of certain persons for particular acts many forces operate to eliminate a high proportion of actual offenders from that group which comes to official attention. Such forces include the efficiency with which the individual commits his offense and protects himself from observation; the availability to the offender of social and personal resources; and the patterns of local law enforcement. Furthermore, many persons are arrested who do not come to trial; and not all who are tried are referred for correctional treatment.

As a result of these social selection processes a high proportion of correctional clients come from socially and economically deprived groups in the community. Effects of the official selection procedures are seen in the various adjustments of the correctional client to the stress inherent in such experiences as arrest, interrogation, detention, and court hearing, and in the expectations which the client brings to his first experiences with the correctional agency.

The implications of this concept for the education of social workers who are to enter correctional services are several. The correctional social worker will need:

Knowledge of:

The nature of the social selection processes which determine which offenders remain unidentified, which are dealt with by other social institutions, and which are committed to correctional caseloads;

The stresses experienced by the client during formal selection processes;

The characteristic defenses against stress evidenced by clients with different backgrounds and personality patterns;

The effect of the social selection process on the initial stages of the client-worker relationship;

The economic and social facts of the lower class culture from which legally identified offenders are largely selected.

Skills in:

Dealing with defenses which have been mobilized by stress experiences;

Identifying strengths and potentialities in persons with habits of personal and social failure and in situations with minimal resources.

Attitudes of:

Respect for and interest in persons who have been progressively rejected by the community;

Acceptance of a role in the administration of criminal justice with its stress-producing procedures in a way which neither condones harshness nor sides with the client against the representatives of law and justice.

SUB-CULTURES

All persons are members of sub-cultures, and it has become a truism in social work that the client's sub-culture affects the way he uses the social worker's service. Understanding something of his values, his means of communication, the patterns of his thought and his accustomed ways of life is essential in helping the client find solutions to his problems.

In work with those deviants who become part of the correctional caseload, three sub-cultures are of importance in addition to the religious, ethnic, and racial sub-cultures which social work has learned to recognize. The first of these is the working class or lower class sub-culture from which many correctional clients come. This sub-culture is often regarded by members of the middle class as delinquent in itself. Its differences are evident in attitudes toward authority, use of money, supervision of children, personal ambition, ways of having fun, physical expression of aggression, and many other human activities. However, these patterns are not necessarily delinquent and many lower class individuals do not become officially identified offenders. The problem for the social worker is to help lower class offenders achieve reasonably conforming behavior without requiring of them impossible and inappropriate middle class patterns of life. Establishing mutual understanding and acceptance between the lower class offender and his middle class community is one of the tasks of the correctional social worker.

A second sub-culture which is of particular importance to the correctional social worker is the delinquent or criminal sub-culture. It is through the groups in this sub-culture that patterns of delinquent behavior are learned. The delinquent or criminal group may be the client's only resource for human warmth, acceptance and status after he has been identified by the community as an offender. This sub-culture has a language of its own, with symbols, rituals, and patterns of relationship which are difficult for the outsider to observe. The groups in this sub-culture are often the strongest force opposed to the value-change which the social worker is attempting to help the client achieve. Learning to know this sub-culture and acquiring the ability to modify its effect on the client's life is one of the most difficult tasks which the correctional social worker faces.

There is still a third client sub-culture which the correctional worker must keep in mind—the correctional sub-culture. Correctional clients have been through an experience which is shared only by other identified offenders. Although these clients may not be directly related to each other, each carries within himself an understanding of what it means to "do time." This correctional sub-culture is particularly well-organized and influential in institutions, where it operates to defeat the change-producing efforts of the staff. Again, this is a sub-culture with a language of its own expressing a set of meanings which the correctional social worker must learn to understand.

In order to give service in the correctional agency the social worker must have:

Knowledge of:
The content of the sub-cultures which have meaning to his clients.

Skills in:
Communicating with persons from sub-cultures which are foreign to his experience;

Devising means by which persons from the lower class culture can achieve acceptable social conformity within patterns based in their cultural experience;

Modifying the groups which have influence on the client's adjustment.

Attitudes of:
Acceptance of difference without loss of personal and professional identity;

Enjoyment of the widely various ways in which human groups express themselves.

ACTING-OUT DISORDERS

Many of the deviants who become correctional clients evidence a variety of "acting-out disorders." This is not an intellectually satisfactory concept. It reports descriptively an empirical classification which invites further study and the development of an adequate typology of sub-classes. It points to a widely reported characteristic of the correctional caseload, the fact that the clients are in general people who act out their feelings and impulses. Present nosological classifications deal with these personalities as neurotic characters, character disorders, sociopaths, or psychopaths. Diagnostic practice varies from agency to agency, and psychiatrists who usually see a highly selected segment of the caseload differ among themselves as to the nature of these difficulties. Social workers who see the entire caseload have found that the acting-out personalities fall into rough descriptive sub-classes which are useful in differentiating treatment but are not adequately formulated for theoretical purposes.

Because these personalities have been less well studied by psychiatry and because many of them do not respond to traditional therapeutic methods, many of them have been considered "untreatable." Yet the correctional social worker is required to do something with them. Because social workers in corrections have unique access to these personalities in action, it may well be that social work has a special contribution to make to diagnostic understanding of the dynamics underlying their behavior.

There are several implications for social work practice when the caseload is largely composed of "acting-outers." Interviews often prove to be limited instruments for securing diagnostically helpful information and must be supplemented by observations of behavior and of interactions with other persons. Such personalities are often limited in the use of verbal communication techniques and communication through action is a primary tool for the worker who would be influential. The way the social worker organizes his work load is often affected by the fact that such clients live in a continuous series of emergencies. Organization of work is affected by these emergencies not only because the worker is responsible to the community to minimize their destructive effects, but also because this sort of personality is often more accessible to influence during and immediately after an emergency than at a later time. It is also true that an emergency which is not quickly dealt with can lead to a crescendo of difficulties which defer the possibility of treatment indefinitely.

Where the primary symptomatology of the clients is "acting-out" the social worker will need:

Knowledge of:
The tentative formulations of the dynamics of such personalities in
   the available diagnostic literature.

Skills in:
Gathering diagnostically useful information through observation of
   behavior and interaction as well as through interviewing techniques;
Communication through action as well as through verbal interchange;

Use of the emergency for treatment purposes;

Flexible and selective organization of work;

Formulation of the findings of practice in a way that will contribute
to the knowledge of the dynamics of "acting-out."

Attitudes of:

Strength, steadiness, directedness and durability as he lives with the
offender through his social difficulties;

Readiness to administer his work load according to a model which
is efficient in management of "acting-out" cases;

Research-mindedness in work with each case.

HANDICAPPED STATUS

Many, perhaps all, clients of social agencies experience a socially
handicapped status in becoming clients. Certain clients are legally
assigned such handicapped status. Every correctional client has
been assigned a specified period of such handicapped status as the
penalty for committing an offense.

The legal and social handicaps inherent in the status of correctional clients are outlined in Chapter I. The implications of this
status for service are found in the client's relationship to the community, in the client's feelings about himself, and in the responsibilities of the social worker for administering the restrictions and
obligations of the status.

In order to discharge these responsibilities and to serve the client
the social worker will need:

Knowledge of:

The legal requirements of the status;

The social and psychological effects of such restrictions on the client;

The means by which the client's success or failure in meeting the
obligations of his status are observed;

The functions of case records in the administration of such a legal
status.

Skills in:

Observing the client's success or failure in meeting his obligations;

Reporting these observations so that they are useful in the legal
decision-making process as well as in the treatment process;

Individualizing the impact of the handicapped status on the client's

life so that he is supported in meeting his obligations and in earn-
ing his return to normal status.

Attitudes of:
Acceptance of the handicapped status as a form of penalty which fits
within our social value system and offers opportunity for reintegration of the offender within the community.

STRESS

All clients experience stress from the circumstances which cause
them to turn to a social agency for help. The correctional client is
characterized by the fact that he has been deliberately subjected to
stress by the community whose values he has violated. The net
result of the process of becoming an officially identified offender is
to dislocate the offender's common patterns of adjustment and to
place him in a special status which requires reorganization of his
ways of life. This is in itself a stressful experience. The social
worker's task is to utilize this experience of dislocation as a stimulus
to achieving new and more useful adjustments.

In order to accomplish this task the correctional social worker
will need:

Knowledge of:
The dynamics of stress.

Skills in:
Observing and dealing with the various defenses against stress presented by the offender group.
Using the stress experience to stimulate the offender in efforts toward
more satisfactory self-organization.

Attitudes of:
Acceptance of socially-induced stress as a means for bringing the
offender to self-awareness and readiness to use help.

AGENCY STRUCTURE AS A DETERMINANT IN SERVICE

All social work services are affected by the agency structure within
which the service is offered. Structural aspects of importance for
the nature of service include: the definition of the social task as-

signed to the agency; the sanctioning systems which govern the agency operation; the functional relationships of the agency with other agencies in the community; the constellation of professional and technical personnel required to perform the service; the definition of the role of the social worker; and the processes of social change which determine agency development.

In the correctional field these aspects of structure are characterized by:

A complicated social assignment which reflects several community purposes toward the client: i.e., punishment, control and treatment.

The active participation of the legal sanctioning system in determining service decisions.

Functional interrelationships of correctional agencies with other agencies in the administration of criminal justice.

A constellation of professional and technical personnel which includes lawyers and sociologists as well as all the helping professions, along with technical groups such as police and custodial personnel in institutions.

A role for the worker which involves legally assigned supervision over the basic social and personal adjustment of the client.

An active process of social change affecting the entire system, the result of increasing social pressure to emphasize the treatment purpose of corrections and increasing participation of the helping professions in the correctional process. Since these social forces impinge differentially on local correctional units, the field is characterized by many outmoded organizational units as well as by many divergent experimental approaches.

The analysis of social structure as it impinges on service requires an understanding of various related concepts:

Sanctioning Systems: All social agencies and their personnel are given authority to discharge certain responsibilties through a number of sanctioning systems. For most agencies at least three such systems are required: the legal system which defines the task and the general means for accomplishing it; the administrative system which is concerned with getting the task accomplished through the work of a number of persons; and the profession which is concerned primarily with values and with the competence of personnel. Some agencies are also responsible to a fourth sanctioning system, the religious, which is responsible for certain additional values.

The legal sanctioning system plays a much larger part in correctional agencies than in most social services. Not only are the agencies authorized by law, but the behavior to be dealt with is defined by law. The roles of most personnel and the status of the client are legally defined. The legal profession provides an important group of personnel necessary for the administration of criminal justice. And legal decisions which affect the nature of service are made about every client.

Multi-Discipline Bureaucracy: The decision-making process in the correctional bureaucracy is characterized by the involvement of personnel with many different backgrounds and skills. Although the legal profession is not usually represented in the personnel of the correctional agency, its representatives are actively related to correctional decisions through roles in the administration of criminal justice, i.e., judges, prosecuting attorneys, defense attorneys. Thus the legal profession with its values, traditions, skills and reference groups is represented in the correctional decision-making team. Sociologists, in research and consultant roles, participate in program planning and in this way influence case-by-case decisions.

Many helping professions are also included in the personnel necessary to accomplish the correctional task, including psychiatrists, psychologists, teachers, medical personnel, and religious advisers. Each of these represents the professional sanctioning system in which he has been socialized. Most such personnel move into roles in the correctional system which are defined in ways not anticipated in their basic professional education and each individual makes his own adaptation to the role. This fact results in difficulty of communication among professional team members and lack of clarity about the distribution of responsibilities. One of the key problems of correctional administrators at this time concerns the integration of various professional personnel into the correctional service.

Other groups of personnel whose decisions have a major effect on service decisions are not organized as professions but make significant contributions in knowledge and skill. Of particular importance among these groups of personnel are the police and the custodial staffs of institutions. One of the characteristics of the decision-making process in corrections is that many of these officially responsible persons have direct relationships with the client and make independent decisions about him. The problem of rationalizing and integrating the decision-making process as it affects the individual client in this sort of culti-discipline bureaucracy is a primary concern in designing effective treatment.

Role of the Worker: Any social worker brings a new role into the constellation of roles with which the client, so long as he remains client, must interact. The definition of the social worker's role has a major impact on what happens to the client. The role definition of any social worker consists of his assigned responsibilities, the means he may use in discharging his responsibilities, and the patterns of relationships which he is expected to follow in work with his clients and his colleagues. All social work roles are defined by the structure of the employing agency as well as by the profession which trained the worker.

The social worker's role in corrections includes some responsibilities and certain means for discharging responsibility which are not found in other social work roles. These include legal responsibility for general supervision of the client's social relationships; responsibility for many decisions which are usually left to the client; and responsibility for using controls over behavior which are based on the force of the state. The social work role in corrections also involves more widely extensive patterns of decision-sharing than do most other social work roles. Furthermore, a characteristic professional sub-culture develops in the correctional agency because of the definition of the role and the characteristics of the caseload with which the correctional social worker is dealing.

In order to adapt social work functioning within this structure of service the social worker will need:

Knowledge of:
The administration of criminal justice seen in historical perspective as a changing social structure reflecting at each stage societal values and technological developments.
The correctional system as a part of the administration of criminal justice.
The interrelationships of various sanctioning systems in determining the responsibilities and means of influence of the correctional service.
The roles and functions of various personnel in the correctional bureaucracy.
The traditions, values, skills, and reference groups of the legal pro-

fession as well as of those professions with which social workers
have been accustomed to work;

The processes of social change now active in the correctional system
and the social policy issues which are crucial to further development.

Skills in:

Discharging the legal responsibilities of the social worker as a part of
the administration of criminal justice;

Use of the legal procedures in a way which protects the client and
structures his experience for learning;

Teamwork with sociologists, lawyers, police and custodial personnel
as well as with various representatives of the helping professions;

Contributing from the role of social worker to agency change in the
direction of improved service to clients.

Attitudes of:

Acceptance of the traditions, functions, values and educational backgrounds of various kinds of personnel;

Willingness to learn from and work with personnel whose contributions differ from that of the social worker;

Acceptance of the need to work with structure as well as with individual relationships in the development of service to clients;

Readiness to be part of a professional sub-culture which is determined by the reciprocal worker-client roles.

AUTHORITY AS A DYNAMIC IN SERVICE RELATIONSHIPS

Authority, which is authorized influence over other persons, is a
fact in every social worker-client relationship. It stems both from
the structure in which the worker has a role and from the profession which has certified his competence. The authority of the social
worker inheres in the position he occupies and defines the area of
responsibility he is expected to assume, the kinds of decisions he
may make, and the means of influence he may use in order to discharge his responsibility. The authority assigned to the social
worker differs from one service program to another, varying according to the kind of client need which is being met, the sanctioning systems involved in the authorization of the service, and the
role definition of the worker. The authority of the worker's position tends to be increased whenever the clients of the agency are

perceived to be dangerous or unable to take responsibility for themselves.

The authority assigned to the social worker's position in the correctional agency is more extensive than in most agencies. It is characterized by:

The legal assignment to the social worker of supervisory responsibility over the client.

The removal from the client of many decisions usually left to the individual with the responsibility for many of these decisions assigned to the social worker.

The extension of permissible means of influence assigned to the worker's position to include controls over behavior which are based on the force of the state.

The worker's responsibility, as a legal authority person in the client's life, to relate with other authority persons responsible for the client, including family members, employers, school personnel, and representatives of other agencies.

Two subsidiary concepts which need elaboration in connection with this analysis—*decision-making* and *control over behavior* have been discussed in some detail in Chapter I.

This kind of an authority position has significant implications for social work in corrections. These include:

The characteristic transference phenomena which appear in the early stages of the relationship with the client.

The emphasis in work with cases and groups on decision-making by both worker and client.

The need for professional skill in using a wide range of controls over behavior.

The worker's responsibility for direct relationship with significant authority persons in the client's life whether in the family or in the community.

In order to discharge the responsibilities of this authority position the social worker needs:

Knowledge of:
The dynamics of social control;
The processes of decision-making.

Skills in:

Analyzing the authority assigned to his particular position so he can
be clear about his area of responsibility, the decisions which he
must make, and the means of influence he may use;

Making the decisions for which he is responsible with reference to
the decisions of other responsible persons and with respect for
procedures of accountability;

Training the client in decision-making;

Dealing with the negative transference components and the associated dependency needs which are precipitated by the imposition
of correctional authority;

Individualizing the use of controls;

Working with many persons in each case as they are affected by and
affect the client's adjustment;

Mobilizing the persons responsible for the client in the community
in support of his efforts to participate normally in the community.

Attitudes of:

A resolution of his own problems with authority which allows him
to use authority constructively rather than punitively or over-
protectively;

Ability to bear the strain of making decisions in a situation in which
the complexities are many, the problems difficult, and the available knowledge limited;

Ability to empathize with more than one person in a given problem
situation.

RESPONSIBILITY FOR VALUE-CHANGE

We have said that the correctional social worker is given authority
in order to change the ways clients express values in action. All
social workers work with their clients in terms of values. Values
impinge on their work through: the community's values as expressed in the authorization of the service; the values which have
been internalized by the worker in the process of professional education; the values which workers hold as individuals; and the
values which are important to the clients. When these sets of values
are in general congruent with each other, the social worker's task
relative to value-change is comparatively simple and is seldom
identified as a professional problem. When the systems of values
held by the community, the profession, the worker, and the client

are diverse or in conflict, then the social worker's task is more difficult.

More than in any other social service, the correctional social worker's task is defined in terms of changing the values of the client so that they become congruent in action with the values of the community. The form of deviance which makes a person a correctional client is defined as an attack on community values, and the goal of service is social functioning which no longer evidences deviant values. The point of view from which the client's values are defined as deviant is essentially middle class. The client's value system is often drawn from lower class experience and is supported by groups with delinquent or criminal value systems.

In achieving the value-change which is required of the client, the social worker's task is made more difficult by the fact that the community values expressed in the authorization of the correctional agency are diverse and sometimes in conflict. Certain groups in the community seek punishment of the client through the correctional agency. Other groups are most concerned that the client be controlled. And increasingly powerful groups are insisting that treatment of the client be the foremost concern. Every correctional agency reflects in some way a compromise among relatively powerful interest groups expressing these different values. These diverse value orientations are also represented in each case by persons who are immediately concerned with the client and his behavior.

An added difficulty for the social worker in corrections stems from the fact that the social work profession has tended to neglect these value problems and has treated certain professional values as absolutes, such as the client's right to self-determination and the non-judgmental approach of the worker, at the expense of other social values, such as the importance to the client and community that destructive behavior be minimized and that respect for the individual includes holding him responsible for his behavior within the limits of his capacity. Thus the values internalized through professional education have often seemed to the worker to be in conflict with those structured within the correctional system. In addition, many social workers are themselves middle class in orientation and unaware that lower class values may be different without being inherently delinquent.

In order to discharge his responsibilities for changing values the correctional social worker will need:

Knowledge of:
The processes by which community values are crystallized in agency structure;
The content of value systems as they appear in the various sub-cultures of our society;
The ways values are expressed and modified;
The effect of efforts to change values on treatment relationships and on group memberships.

Skills in:
Differentiation between deviant values which can be expressed without danger to the person or the community and those deviant values which must be modified in order to preserve membership in the community;
Differentiation between behavior which fails to meet community standards because of inability to perform according to values, and that behavior which arises out of values which are in conflict with community standards;
Communication with persons with various value systems;
Helping the client internalize those values which are necessary for adequately socialized behavior;
Helping the client deal with the effect of value-change on his group relationships;
Participating in the processes by which his agency modifies service structure in line with professional values.

Attitudes of:
Ability to resolve the value conflicts which are built into the correctional system in a way which permits action and does not undermine professional integrity.

THE INSTITUTION AS A TOOL IN TREATMENT

Many fields of social service use institutions as one means of providing necessary care for clients. In the correctional field many clients experience both institutional care and service from field agencies. For corrections the institution is important both as a means of protecting the community against further depredations by known offenders and as a means of breaking old patterns of behavior and substituting new ones. Increasingly the institution in corrections is being perceived, not as a place where the client can be held while he is given clinical treatment, but as itself a tool of treatment. This idea of the institution as an important change-producing instrument is relatively unexplored but offers much promise for the reeducation of offenders. Such a use of the institution requires that the social worker have knowledge of social structure as it affects behavior as well as skill in modifying social structure. It suggests a new role for social workers in the institution, which involves knowledge and skill in relation to both individuals and groups.

In order to participate in the developing concept of institutional treatment the social worker needs:

Knowledge of:
The dynamics of the inmate culture;
The interrelationship of formal institutional structure and the formation of the inmate culture.

Skills in:
Work with groups as well as with individuals;
Designing aspects of formal structure so that the institution provides reeducative experiences for the client;
Work with many kinds of personnel toward a common treatment goal.

Attitudes of:
Readiness to redesign social work roles in the interest of maximized service to clients.

IMPLICATIONS FOR THE SOCIAL WORK CURRICULUM

The objectives identified in this study of social work practice in corrections has several implications for the social work curriculum.

1. *No separate speciality seems required in order to prepare social workers to take their place in correctional service.* The basic

social work approach to service is uniquely appropriate for dealing with the human problems which are presented in the correctional assignment. Enrichment of the curriculum, however, is needed if social workers are to be as ready to enter correctional employment as any other field of service.

2. *The social work task in corrections seems to call for social workers rather than for caseworkers or group workers.* All social workers in corrections work with individuals, groups and communities, with less emphasis on the use of one method than is characteristic of many social work jobs.

3. *Social science concepts are of particular importance in preparing social workers to understand the correctional caseload and to work within the correctional agency.* Such concepts include those of deviance, structure, status, role, authority, and sub-culture.

4. *The study of practice in corrections has much to contribute to social work theory and to the education of all social workers.* Concepts of use to all social work which are particularly well illustrated in correctional social work include: social selection of caseload, handicapped status, acting-out disorders, stress, structure as a determinant in service, role of worker, decision-making, use of controls over behavior, authority as a dynamic in service relationships, the problems of value-change, and the institution as a tool in treatment.

5. *The present stage of development in correctional services calls for social workers who can contribute as leaders to social policy and to advancing knowledge.* The profession itself can play a strategic role in the design of correctional treatment, and the career line of social workers in corrections leads rapidly into positions of research, demonstration, and administration. Professional education should select and prepare students for early leadership responsibility.